JOYRIDING TO NIGHTFALL

Joan Colby

FUTURECYCLE PRESS
www.futurecycle.org

Cover artwork, "Halloween Ghouls Joyriding in Truck" by Marilyn Gould; author photo by C. Bennorth Photography; cover and interior book design by Diane Kistner; Carlito text and Copperplate titling

Library of Congress Control Number: 2019932560

Published by FutureCycle Press
Athens, Georgia, USA

ISBN 978-1-942371-76-2

CONTENTS

—

—

—

YOU DON'T NEED A WEATHERMAN TO KNOW
WHICH WAY THE WIND BLOWS.

—BOB DYLAN

BEFORE THE WEATHER MOVES UPON US

Smudged to the south, the sky portends
Wind and rain, though for now
A perfect stillness hangs over the garden
As it must have before a question was raised,
A want expressed, something juicy tasted.
Philosophy has no truck with weather.
The silent flowers emanate
A sweetness beyond language. The deer sleep
In a wood where doctrine
Never browses. These are tales we design
To savor existence. A woman rising from the sea.
A man upholding the world
On massive shoulders. How every child that is born
Is born to save us.

ICE STORM IN DECEMBER

Through binoculars, I see the door to the barn
Slightly ajar; the hook hanging so I know
You're out there, presumably safe
Despite the storm with its freezing bullets
And sixty-mile winds out of the east.

You could have fallen, be lying right now by the black mare's
Stall with a broken hip like Wally when the colt reared.
The iced air could have brought on
A heart attack. You could be gasping your last as I wonder
If I should put on boots and parka and head out there.

When is it time to decide? Last week, Win's daughter
Waited two days, her phone call unanswered.
She found him on the bathroom tiles,
His body temp down to 92 degrees.

The red-bellied woodpecker is at the suet block
Stabbing like mad as the feeder swings
In the morning's mayhem. And you emerge,
Plodding slowly up our lane so I can see
How every step is a heft of will, scarf pulled
Across your face, like a burglar set to break in
To the house of the winds.

JANUARY FOG

Fog grips the house with pale gloves
Like a long-ago woman dressed for visitations.
Mid-January, what snow remains
Is dingy as a book of lies.
Revise the calendar to
Cornstubble where geese throng
The easy pickings, where a freezing rain
Begins to ice the power lines.
It seems like forever, days like these
When there's no reason to celebrate,
No music canting its grace notes,
No sweet talk, no curses.
People of faith speak to ghosts.
A friend gets testy defending UFOs,
Citing a schoolyard of children, two Japanese
Pilots. It's better, I suppose,
Than what I think, which is nothing.
Like an evil spirit, the fog
Swallows our road.

FEBRUARY THAW

Darkness coils in the melt field beneath the silver maple
Whose divided trunk extends great limbs
Like the Star of David or a composition for six voices.

The sky it reaches for is plated
With a dull patina like pewter
Or the cheap silverware acquired with coupons.

The old snow oozes into a common element,
The singularity of its crystals lost to an
Embossed drip where icicles incline, ragged daggers.

The shallow roots hump like thirsty serpents.
Tonight, the Crow Moon rises. The dark plain: Sinus Aestuum
Calls to the wolves mating, to the blackbirds hunched on branches.

A farewell note is written in the jittery frost
Of a window framed in dimming lamplight.
Written. Written and delivered.

EVE OF THE DAY

In the far north, in the darkened hours
When the light is snuffed
Like a candle
And you gather near the hearth
Of the storyteller and listen
So intently your heart blazes up
In a celebration of sparks,
It is then
You learn to hope beyond the cold stars
The runes foretold. So new stories
Replace old stories. Gods disembark
From dragonships as the child of peace
Walks barefoot through the snow.
Does it matter what you believe
If the light returns, if the days
Stretch out their little hands
With bouquets of everlasting?
Burn the great log by the sea
And fit the new words
To the old war songs:
How the people have always stood
Together while the neon skies rave,
Counting on some promise made
Ages ago,
Improvised and polished like the touchstone,
Like the torches dipped in oil,
The child swaddled on the cradleboard.

IN EVERY WALK WITH NATURE, ONE RECEIVES
FAR MORE THAN HE SEEKS.

—JOHN MUIR

BLACKFLIES

They descend in umbrellas of trouble.
The foxhound howls, rolling in the grass,
Her belly thick with feeding specks.

Shuddering, a man in waders
Reels in his line. The sky darkens.
He seizes his creel, the fish crawling with marauders.

It is the singular mammal that makes the news.
The bear attack. The mountain lion. But it's the pests
Small and voracious we learn to dread.

In a marriage, it's not the definitive fight
That is to blame, but the little persistent bites
Until the back of the neck is one red welt,

Until even the eyelids swell,
The hands measled, the scourged belt
Of flesh between pantsleg and sock.

When they arrive in a blanket of woe,
You drop the camera and run for the truck
Swearing you'll never be back

In a season like this, how the vows you meant
On the beautiful afternoon are moot
Now that the wind has lifted them

Into the story,
Now that the trunk
Has been opened and everything loosed.

RIME

Ice fog embellishes the morning trees
In rime, a frozen tranquility
The sun will banish in an hour.
So brief, this curious beauty
Of imminence and loss,
Like unsustainable passion,
The taste of wild honey on the tongue,
A peregrine's stoop exhausting the blue
Atmosphere, the star shape of the hand,
How the world at last disappears,
Melting in a final exhalation.

LAMB

Greek Easter. The lamb
Is turning on the spit,
Its blood on the lintel
To spare the oldest child.
The sacrifice of Abraham,
Gift to Zeus. *Behold the Lamb
Of God.* The lamb that totters
After Mary, unschooled,
Shorn of will, a perfect follower,
Imprimatur of the spirit.
Its noun: *obedience.* Its verb: *gambol.*
The lamb is patient,
Held in the crook
Of initiation, raised as a host
Above the decorated altar.
Lilies surround it.
Lamb chops sizzle on the grill.
The lamb born into straw
Finds its feet and suckles
The sins of the world.

SPEAKING TO BEES

Bees dislike consternation;
They go peacefully about their tasks.
Each knows its obligation
To the hive: Feeding the queen who loves them
If love is the gift of life.

Bees resent disturbance,
Sudden traffic or an unspoken
Quarrel that troubles the air
In which the bees pursue sweetness.

Take care to be calm
For the sake of bees who dislike anger
But are easily angered, an irony
That would mystify bees in their
Pursuit of simplicity.

Go veiled among bees like women
Who donate their sons to history, like nuns
Who honor silence. Once the bees
Offer their trust, you can walk
Naked in their realm unstung
Like this woman who talks to bees
In a quiet, confiding tone.
She tells them everything,
Not just who has died.

The bees uphold the world
With perpetual industry.
The collapse of hives is like
A vast caldera erupting
In a cloud that might cancel sunlight
For generations.

Remember the man in the woods
Clothed in bees.

When he screamed, his mouth
Choked with the buzzing.
The hoofbeats of his vanishing horse
Echoed the intrusion—
Cantering under the trees
As the bees swarmed
With their new militant queen.

Each hive houses three thousand bees,
A fervent alchemy,
A corporation of golden souls
Entombing their plunder in wax,
A museum of everything we hold
Precious—the pollinated world
In which millions of people are kissing.

WASP

The wasp buzzing, darting.
Your palm covers the sugared glass.
Imagine swallowing such
Malevolence. Throat
A canyon of tribulation in which
A flash flood devises its path
Until you are an inversion
Within an inversion, incapable
Of breath, an avalanche
Blocking the swallow's
Mechanism. This imagination
Is groundless. The wasp
Doodles the garbage can's
Cockeyed lid. How is it
That every occasion becomes
An occasion of sin or temptation
To envision the worst.
Or the sin of omission,
Failing to avert
What you knew or should have known
—as a legal document infers—
For example leaving a pitcher
Of sweetness on the patio
To lure imposter ladybugs.
Their small orange boats overturned.
They smell of rust or disappointment.
The wasp returns
To an investigation of your surplus,
A fearsome saxophone. A jittery
Eighth note, restless and persistent.

THE SQUIRREL

Just one time, the squirrel succeeded
In launching from the birdbath
To the top of the feeder where he gobbled
Suet studded with sunflower seeds
Like a man hit by a car gulps the offered brandy
And thanks Providence despite a broken femur.

The squirrel, obviously also injured,
Limped off as I clapped my hands
The way God is said to do when annoyed,
Flooding the earth with a demand
To be adored. Each day the squirrel contemplates
The consequence of sin, sits up poised
On the edge of the stone birdbath
Upheld by three cherubim,
And folds his hands over his belly
Like Buddha, wondering about the worth
Of relinquishing desire.

Opossum

Grin full of teeth,
Narrow white mask,
Eyes chambered as bullets,
Crouched over the barn cats'
Kibble. Naked prehensile tail.
Here are some facts:
Bifurcated penis or vagina.
Pouch for the young.
Immune to pit vipers.
Omnivorous. Solitary. Edible
If you are hungry enough.

When threatened, an involuntary
Collapse. Slobbered grimace,
Foul smell of the death
It impersonates. Stiff with a
Rigor mortis
I'm not fearsome enough
To engender.

Looks at me. Face of
A ratlike monk whose prayer
Is *Fill this good bowl*
Daily, for I have come.

MITES

Article and photos from *The National Geographic*

The oribatid soil mite is a one-man band,
A Rube Goldberg concoction.
Green, orange, purple, pink,
Grotesque with a bluster of tendrils. Devilishly
Clever as the curse or blessing
Of evolution.

Mites devour bugs, promote infection
In a dog's ear. They mount
Tanks of army ants. Eat their
Mothers. Plow the earth like peasants.
Specialists of design and
Advantage, their preferred habitats
Are bodies.

In horror, I read they fuck upon my
Face while I am sleeping. Attain a brief
Adulthood, lay eggs in follicles
I carefully soap and cream.
They fill up with shit and die
On my head, their chosen globe.

O, dreadful microscopic lives!
That sci-fi notion: how we might exist
As microbes on the eyelash of God.
Forgive our sins,
Monster trucks, ghastly helmets, gargoyles of
An ulterior civilization. How could we believe that love
Is our salvation.

PHOTOS FOUND IN CAMERA

Grizzly in a high meadow
Looks bovine, head down, grazing
On what—groundberries, herbs, particular
Grasses. Or something small and dead.
Bears, like men, omnivorous.

Next shot, closer, focused on a
Patch of green. The grizzly raises
His head, scenting. Doglike snout, piggy
Eyes, red-brown as an animated
Shag rug. Captured in a moment
Of bemused suspicion.

Back at the meal now, he's busy,
Bigger, biting something. Teeth and claws
At work, a bit nearer you'd see
The discoloration like a stained
Document. What a forefather.
Large, male, solitary.

With a few audacious steps,
The zoom nails his massive jaws. Conjecture:
An almost visible huff. Face up, peering.
Something dripping from the jowls.

Final frame: slightly out of focus.
Rearing like a giant from
A Grimm story. Battery of teeth,
Tactical, armed.
Mouth wide open.

Gator

They told Dad that if he'd lasso the gator they'd
Remove it. Only fair, since the gator was here
Before dad ever built the house on the canal.

The gator lurked by the trash can. It could outrun
A pig, Dad always contended, not to mention a 75-
Year-old man even though he played

Tennis daily and did the Swedish
Calisthenics he'd practiced since
Boyhood. He grew up with gators,

Coral snakes and panthers. It wasn't like he
Wasn't as much a native. He, too, was a
Gator, class of '21, Phi Beta Kappa.

Some people put out kibble
For the gator so it went right to the
Source and ate their dog.

Only Yankees, Dad thought,
Would be that stupid. He was pissed off
With Fish and Wildlife—

Gators in the water-hazard; you
Couldn't retrieve a golf ball.
A man of 75 can't wrestle

A gator, he gets angina just
Thinking how fast a gator
Can run (faster than a wild boar—

Whoever measured that, I wonder). Finally
He moved to a condo in a gated
Community with a bunch of

Leathery old gators who lounged
In the sun, eyes hooded with the deceptive
Patience of the reptile.

THE OLD FERAL CAT

We build straw castles for the old cat
Secured in the winter barn now that
His companion was taken by the coyotes,
A scream across night fields last year. Our vote
Was for salvation. Now the orange feral I call
Scout and you call Cat lives in a stall
Filled with golden bales and blankets, a bed
With a fuzzy lining. But he likes to shed
The provenance of civilized existence
To crouch against a frosty pane where his persistence
Grants no liberty. We bring bottles of warm
Water, fill the automatic feeder with a swarm
Of Senior kibble, Toss a handful of the treats
He favors. Here within his solitary suite
No canine incisors can grip him as he stalks
The birds or shrews, hovering like the hawks
That cruise the updrafts. Byron wrote of this;
How in Chillon the prisoner found the bliss
Of relinquishing everything, even hope.
The cat measures amplitude: the scope
Of walled territory, the occasional field mouse
That wiggles in to find his claws
Unsheathed, as when he slunk along
The fencelines, ready to disable song.
We praise the lack of slaughtered feathers.
How we have saved him from savage weathers
Too cold or hot for his aging bones.
We fondle him, insisting he's not alone,
Though our touch is what he merely endures.
His topaz eyes fixed on the beguiling swerve
Of shadow as we enter and go out
Careful as politicians armed with the clout
Of his confinement foremost in our care.
So he cannot be taken unaware.

O Scout or Cat, nameless wild one, it took years
To tolerate our custody, our ruthless fears
That preserve you from whatever fate
Lurks in the woodlot, beyond the gate
We guard as if your salvation in this stone
Mausoleum could ensure our own.

SIGNATURE RERUM

—Jacob Boehm

This is the language of nature
Whence everything speaks out of its property.

The bifurcated manroot prized
As an aphrodisiac, hunted
In the hills of Appalachia.

Signature stands in the essence

As a rhino's horn restores
Sexual prowess.

Inward form is noted in outward form
As in a beast, an herb and trees.

The overwintering liver leaf,
Its dried blood hue signifying
A tea for hepatic ills.

Everything as it is inwardly
And outwardly signed.

The rattlesnake master,
Foliage like a diamondback's
Addendum. A snakebite cure...
How many died in that belief?

Evil to good, good to evil, it has
Its external character.

Similarities root in the brain's hardpan.

Nothing that is created or born in nature,
But it also manifests its internal
Form externally.

Thus: the beautiful woman must be
Pure. The noble profile denotes
Wisdom. The sly eye is a thief.
In such lordly pronunciations,
Mankind embraced grief.

Nature in its form is a dumb essence.

LANIAKEA—IMMEASURABLE HEAVENS

Here we are in the confectionary of the Milky Way,
One of a hundred thousand galaxies,
An immense pharmacy where
A hundred million billion suns
Dispense the elements of sweetness,
The acid components of despair.

We float in the Virgo supercluster,
Children of an immaculate conception,
The mechanisms that conspired the air
Our primitive gills learned to love.

Our bodies imitate the way
Tendrils of the cosmic web connect the nodes
So nerve and muscle let us rise
To walk the finite earth that flows,
Inexorably fueled by a dark force,
To the basin called The Great Attractor.

'

TULIPS

Wood turtles stamp the ground
Like infuriated children to lure
Earthworms, a special treat
Along with slugs, snails and other slimy
Delectables. I feel like stamping
When I observe how he has dug up
The tulip bulbs from a long-established bed,
Scarlet and golden every May,
Because, he says, their bloom is brief;
Then there's just these greeny spears,
As if warriors left a jungly mess.
He wants all-summer color,
Perennial substance, asks me
If there are varieties of tulips
That bloom through August.
Listen, spring is defined with tulips, crocus,
Iris, jonquils, birdsong for God's sake.
That bracelet of velvet tulips.
Black tongues silenced by ignorance.
I think of the neighbor who cut down
A two-hundred-year-old white oak
So an above-ground plastic pool
Could take its place; of the people
Who claim climate change is
A myth, who explain what God
Has in mind (at least
For them), who entertain
Notions of trapping wolves and wild
Horses, who lower the educational bar
So everyone can pass and the world
Can be ruled by idiots. So I can rant
Like a madwoman: O wood turtles
Come out and drum the land
Senseless until the worms
Rise in a slithery mass,
Until everyone understands
The necessity of tulips.

THE HARDER THE CONFLICT, THE MORE GLORIOUS
THE TRIUMPH.

—THOMAS PAINE

STAND UP FOR THE STUPID AND CRAZY

—Walt Whitman

Give five bucks to the woman with the sign
And the four homeless children and the hungry dog.
Even if it's a scam, as everyone insists, it's still a hell of a way
To make a living.

And the guy wandering along the riverbank
Talking to himself. Let him be.
It's a free country, and if he wants to throw himself
Into the river tonight, that's his choice.

If someone spends the grocery money
On a lottery ticket, let him. He just might win
And even if he doesn't he had that hope,
Which is as good as hot dogs or Mountain Dew.

And if a girl is screaming in the restroom
Because her boyfriend killed her cat,
Scream right along with her, you'll
Both feel better. Then help her kick his ass.

So go ahead and do something willfully stupid.
Buy that pot of flowers with your last ten dollars.
Forget the electric bill. Who needs lights
When you can go crazy and samba in the streets?

KNEECAPPED

> Mr. White to Mr. Orange: In terms of pain,
> go for the knee, worse than the stomach.

"It's a mother-fucker," says Derek my therapist
Urging me to bend. "90 degrees," he demands. Last week
Was 85, next he'll want 100. He's never satisfied.
Two horns of the implant; under the skin, wires
Like narrow eels, their fierce eyes glaring
From the cavern of pain. A figure eight
Within a square: symbol for extinction.
The surgical term: fixation. Stable
Unless it shifts like the fault
Of New Madrid that reversed the father of rivers.
The IRA chose it as a fitting
Punishment for traitors. To live in pain,
Unbending as an atheist when the priest
Compels the congregation. I will not kneel
To confess my sins or whisper
Through the grill where God's lieutenant
Languishes in boredom, dispensing Hail Marys
As if a game could be won so easily.
As if blowing things up could change
The matrix of violence. As if accidents
Don't simply happen. When the dog
Bashes into me wanting to play,
My husband says "We might as well rename her
Goddamn." He hopes to curtail
The curses I've grown fond of; I read they make
A person happier. The surgeon observed proudly
How my knee was a challenge to reconstruct.
It's a son of a bitch, that's what it is,
The sliding patella like a gun being cocked,
Clasped by a tendon that grips the quadriceps
The way an assassin garrotes a victim.
I strap the weights on my ankle and kick
While Derek waves his measuring stick
Like an avenging angel.

MIGRAINE

Like a tsunami it rears
Over the left orbital beach.

A small bucket in the jeep
For the riptide of nausea.

Fog thickens in the bleak sea-cave
Of heritage. Father gripped his temples and paced.

The Egyptians drilled the skull
So demons might flee.

Scribonius Largus placed
An electric ray on the brow.

Luigi Galvani built a machine
To electrify headaches, alcoholism, neurasthenia.

The black fish of migraine spawns
In the river behind the eyeball.

Lie down. Be still.
Make friends with darkness.

REFLECTIONS AFTER MIDNIGHT

Full moon and one bat diving for insects.
You sit in the tree of wonder
Drinking scotch and remembering
How the red eye of a cigarette
Could stab the darkness,
The languor after sex,
Smoke ascending in perfect zeros.

Somewhere a dog is barking
The monotony of boredom.
An owl's hoodoo phrase,
Coyotes on the hunt,
Their ragged xylophones
Along the creekbed.

This tree leaning awkwardly as a crutch
Must come down. Your mind's a chainsaw,
Your thoughts troubling
As nightjars. How in childhood
The mother is memory, the father
Resolution. And you—fount of confusion
Watching the sky stitched with the spangled
Myths of your forefathers.

Ice melts in your glass, weary and loveless.
The house is dark, its windows closed.
A long walk from here to there
With only the moon's frail reflection.

COMPOSING THE ESSAY

The first rule is to narrow the topic
So love becomes unspeakable
As voices buzzing
At the hives of God.

Parse the big sentences
Of justice or mercy
Into soulless abstractions.

Fondle one small creature,
The ferret of imagination
Or the snowy owl of changing weathers,

And you will learn that
When the heart fails
Everything fails.

Sheep and goats: the first domesticated.
Lamb of God or Satan's spawn.
Shepherds model patience. Abel
On a hillside watching quietly—such virtue
Is seldom rewarded. The sheep offers
Its throat to the knife. The goat,
Laden with sin, is driven out.

The willow and the poppy,
From these Hoffmann synthesized
Aspirin, then heroin. What we want is to be soothed,
Fevers subdued, desires obliterated,
Or else we want to shoot through space
On a tongue of flame. The self drifting
Like Pangaea split or dividing like
Comb jellies. Obeisance, divine mother
Of nerves.

Abel holds the orphan lamb
Like a blessed gift. Cain seethes.
Brothers love and brothers kill.
You can never domesticate the wildebeest
Or the wolverine.
Hiroshima was not a myth.
The moon rises so lovers may see
The face of otherness.
Seeking immortality, the Chinese
Invented gunpowder.

A World of Sadness

You will not be sad in this world
Though all the music haunts
Hills garbed in fog, though lilies
Fade in their turquoise vases.
The slow water passes languorously
Beneath the ancient wharf.

A woman on a bench clasps her hands.
The book unopened. The lost poem
Written by a slave whose tongue was severed
For telling how it felt: this loneliness.

Acknowledge the red knob of the closed door.
The broken window where a child peers
Into a littered alley. The rags of dream
You gather to knot about your throat.

Renounce sadness, that old bicycle
Whose wheels no longer revolve,
Those brakes that seize pitching you
Into a pool of milk.

Adorn yourself with the black silks
Of all the midnights spent weeping.
It is not loss so much as
Safekeeping. The locket congealed
With starshine. The opal rings
Of your governing planet
Saturnine, ironic,
As you trouble yourself denying
The sadness that hoods
The visible world.

MEASURE FOR MEASURE

The bubble defines balance.
How wall or floor
Can defy slope. How straight
Trumps meander. The way things fit
Or don't. When it is off,
Words jab with awkward
Swerves; white lies are still untrue.

Quicksilver globes discover the
Body's heat, what's normal
And what's absurd.
The seesaw of morality.

The level holds the spirit,
Heady as a visionary,
Letting a poem bubble to the surface,
Accurate in its constancy
As a lover in the first degrees
Of passion. All these measures
Are dependent on sensitivity.
How the spirit speaks. How mercury
Dazzles in wingtips.

PROBABILITIES

Oil shine behind the door to happiness.
Dull patina of old keys.

A dirt road leads into the foothills,
Jackpine and spruce.

A jay's harsh call.
The flash flood of memories.

What you remember are those
Imagoes of empty streets.

A diner with old men
In overalls forking eggs.

Talk of weather and crops.
Exhaust of a Harley

Hitting the switchbacks.
Fields and fields you once flew over,

Patterns of prosperity or loss.
The scalped mountains of extraction.

A woman in jeans with a yellow dog.
Listen. You have to reach.

POWER

When it fails, you fumble in the dark
For a candle stub and a match.
The furnace grows cold
As a faithless lover.
You open the book of wisdom
To find words blurred
Like melting snow. The doors
Of technology shut on
Entertainment. At dawn, the winter birds
Flock to the feeders. The day proceeds
With its lacks. You huddle at the hearth
Warming your hands. How humble you've become,
Imagining the perk of the coffee pot
Or the jubilant flush of a toilet. Deep
In its pit, the well is silent
As a dwarf whose tongue has been severed.
Consider the communion of bodies,
The society of the pure in heart. Recite
The canticle of the dispossessed
Until a flash of light
And the house groans into its
Accustomed industry. It takes so little
To empower your spirit. To forget.

LEAP

Over the sage, the pronghorn scrawls
Its cursive signature. Fleeing or simply enjoying
The bounce the way speculators rejoice in the
Market's surge. Like a hummingbird, energy vibrating
In the magic of propulsion. Listen, there's a need
To add something extra. The day the Gregorian
Calendar demanded. In Greece, an omen
Of failed marriage while Sadie Hawkins ladies
Compose their proposals. The way a mountain lion
Sails from a high rock to clutch
The sorrel mare's withers as if it could be love
Instead of hunger. The way a poem risks
Misunderstanding, its oblique similes,
Its take-a-dares, its dream.
Like Nijinsky stalled in pure air.

FLOATING

A floating world of guys and dolls,
The crapshoot enterprise of thrown dice.
Woodcuts of tsunamis and Kabuki
Villains. Three beauties and Nathan Detroit
Smoke opium in dreamy pipes.
The fat woman floats in the pool;
Her rich flesh defies gravity.
A hawk floats over the moorland.
Voices float from adjoining tables
Where gossip lures, luminescent
As will-o'-the-wisps. The earth floats
Toward the oblivion
Of its generous star. Time floats
Complicated fingers on the harps
Of galaxies. The water lilies
Seem to float upon Matisse's pond
Yet are anchored with a mass of roots,
The subterranean otherworld he imagined
Over and over and over.

PADRAIG

Mist-laden turf to derby dream,
Trajectory of hope and deceit.

Come on, Come on! As head to head
They hit the wire. He's live

In the daily double. A trifecta
Of fortune like the pot of gold

The shillelagh, the old
Country blarney.

Stake after stake. The charts
Moving up. Impressive wins.

Elephant juice or dope,
Whatever enhancement speed

Demands. Ruled off. Hiding out.
Sleeping rough.

Peddling overpriced
Vacuum cleaners. What a

Come down. Deported as an
Undesirable Irishman. Horse-

Whispering talent and old
Sod magic (*meth, coke, heroin*).

Smiling eyes, clever hands.
O he was a one with the horses.

WHEN THE SAINTS GO MARCHING

The two Johns are being canonized.
It's like a double wedding,
White and gold. The square is jammed
With pilgrims who pay to witness.
I think of the poor the new pope
Advertises, but the poor also yearn
For cathedrals, for the jeweled glass soldered
With lead, the heavy and saturnine element.

Saints were once declared by proclamation,
Martyred in their faith, there was no doubt.
Now rules govern ceremonies. It's said a million
Dollars is required to investigate the
Qualifications. Two miracles prerequisite, yet
To be clear, one John lacks the second cure
Of a terminal patient. That's being fudged
For a dual celebration, as so much has always been.
Science will never squelch
Faith. We want our scapulars, missals and litanies,
The lifted chalice of transubstantiation. The penitents
Crawling to the shrine bearing roses.

When my uncle was made a monseigneur, he purchased
Expensive robes and went to Rome
Where the Holy Father blessed him.
After mass, we'd count the collection haul
At the dining room table. He was locally famous
For building schools and churches. An avid baseball fan,
He had the first satellite dish in town. He drove
A Cadillac and wore his roman collar on vacations
In case he was stopped for speeding. Addressing students,
He displayed a paddle called the Board of Education.
He was acting bishop after the old one died, but turned down
A permanent appointment, not wanting to move
To Great Falls. He was a good man and I suppose
Religious, silently reading his breviary every evening
Before his favorite TV shows came on.

So that's religion, perfectly human,
Full of fault and trickery, but hoping also
To do good—or even be good,
Though that is harder. In a small town in Italy,
A huge wooden cross topples and kills
A passerby. One who believes in omens
Might consider the missing miracle,
How nobody but Jesus was ever credited
With raising the dead.

I feel sacrilegious in these flimsy ironies,
How the stickers of faith pasted on the baptized child
Cling as if an EKG is to be performed
To measure the activity of the heart.
A heart that logic tells me is mechanical,
Not sutured to the sacred breast of Christ
In the bad painting over my mother's bed.
St. Francis Xavier said "Give me the child
Until the age of seven, and he is mine forever."
I shake my head stuffed with information
About the cosmos. Compelled to wear the hair-shirt
Of the agnostic with its intolerable itch.

Meanwhile, the two Johns are rising
In an immaculate hand-hold. Twins
Of a blessed certainty flying up into
The Calendar of Saints.

VOYAGEUR

As a child, he stammered, his face reddening
To choke on a maddening syllable. He learned
Strategies, but still words stood like pickets
At the boundaries of speech. He was a junior
The year of the reenactment. Chewing leather
For moccasins, sewing homespun shirts and
Tasseled caps, constructing the canoes, carving
Paddles, to set out through the Great Lakes like LaSalle
Singing songs of the voyageurs.

It was the worst Midwestern winter in history. The river
Froze. They had to drag their gear 527 miles. During
One portage, a boy was struck and killed
By a semi. That seemed ironic. They forged on
Sleeping in tents at 20 below. *It was so cold, I ached,*
He said. They felt it mainly after they'd been warmed
Indoors performing at towns along the Mississippi. When he sang
The French chanties with the other voyageurs,
The sounds flowed smoothly from his larynx
Like the current of the great river
Carrying him south into the man he would become.
Eight months later they arrived in New Orleans. His father said
You'll never be intimidated now by anything.

Years later, he had a ticket on the Virgin Enterprise,
Which crashed on a test flight in the desert. Undeterred,
He's booked for the Voyager—the name an omen—
Remembers how it was to try to speak
And fail, to shove the heavy canoes into the mighty waters
And paddle on, singing.

Sources

The river eddies into a pit bull's grin,
A too-wide lavish menace.
Love you so much you'll be
Sorry. Sweat bees annoy
The afternoon. Somebody
In a hammock sings
The low-down blues. A wood
Chipper eating the hand
That feeds the poor. A little
Goes a short way; you've got it
Wrong again. Those old shoes
On the back porch useless
As a smashed piñata. The news
Falls out of the sycamores.
Drink the rain and change.

THE WOLVES NEED YOU

Email from The Defenders of the Wolf

My wolf brothers snarled
And kissed my hands.

I wolfed down
Nothing but books.

The wolf loved the redhead.
Ate the grandmother. Huffed
At the pigsty. Teeth white
As the month of December.

The timber wolf in the Top of the World
Zoo in Red Lodge. His yellow eyes.
Brother. Brother.

Old manuscripts
Altered to disguise
Those wolf bitches in the Berlin zoo.

Wolves track you through the steppe
As you flee in your troika. The moon
Belongs to them. No wolves
Have been seen here for years.

OBLIQUE

A fossil captured in amber
Where the pirates of time
Demand ransom. The apparel

Of the hillsides drawn in black ink
As darkness evolves
In the wild grape and sumac.

A basket of napkins that fall
Onto the lawn where a picnic
Is being laid out.

One blink and a dog races across
A meadow. Fixed on prey, it will not
Obey. So that's that.

The motionless swing on the porch.
A Luna moth pasted
Against the screen.

MESSAGES FROM THE LATITUDES OF ILLNESS

You are far away in the city by the lake
That has been frozen all this sad winter,
Boats held hostage, the ghosts of frost
Invigorating the occasional jogger.

How can I reach you in the turmoil
Of artifice? What direction can be pursued?
A circle of peasant women clasp their hands
In their aprons. They have brought fruit
And cabbage soup to assuage you. This one,
Your grandmother, speaks in Ukrainian,
Tells us all will be well in the village of health.

Birds are returning; their voices inhabit
The clouds of morning. I leave you
To the ablutions of nuns without faces,
Their beads a metronome. You are cloistered
In their love.

At the racetrack, I sit in the stands
Clutching my tickets. Here comes the favorite,
Charging around the far turn,
Now bearing out, bolting, riderless, ascending
The tiers to fall upon me like a passion,
Broken legs thrashing, eyes white with terror.

Stunned, I reach for salvation, but no one can help me.
A stranger hands me a gun, says do what you must.
This lovely damaged animal that I must kill and I
Will, I will.

What else can happen? The keys I have lost are found
In the basket of daisies. The book is open
To the passage where Spinoza says
The wise man focuses on life. Darkness crawls
Into the forsythias. The moon recollects its progressions.

ARSON

A swizzle stick of fury stirs
The act, the match, the cask
Of gasoline, sharp as an insult
With its intoxicating scent.
To burn the witch is
Destiny, the torches of the Iroquois
Teasing the captive priests to blaspheme
Or raise their voices in prayer
To the deaf god of the foreigner.
The building sleeps in the humid night,
Its broken fire escapes and alarms,
Blocked doorways of the poor in spirit.
Revenge is red as a flame's first spark.
The children wake to smoke that creeps
Like a fusty rodent beneath the sills.
The three-month baby whimpers, seized
In the father's burning arms. The leap
Into darkness three floors down.
A witness says that, earlier,
A quarrel broke out. Handful of tinder
As the words crisscrossed
In a wigwam bonfire. Nobody thought
It would come to this. She clasps her
Arms to ward off spells.
The bloody tumbrils in the streets
As pelted stones strike their mark.
The quiet grease of women's hymns.
The killing floors. The bundled pyre.
What fire consumes cannot be found.
The children in their simple beds
Of genesis. The bird of fire
Arising from its nest of ash.

PRESENCE

Without absence, presence
Cannot be appreciated. As we say
Sorry for your loss, what we mean is to
Honor your presence in this grief.
To outlive our parents is the natural order.
Today a year-old child sitting in a moving car
Was shot in the head by a stray bullet. Today
You bury your mother who died at 92.
There is no way to measure sorrow
Despite rationalizations of
Addition or subtraction. There are only clichés
Of time and healing, all relative. Our neighbor
Planted a pine tree in memory of his father,
Then ComEd sheared it to a monstrosity
Of anguish. Perhaps that's what is meant
In the long scheme we talk of
Knowledgeably as savants who recite
One thing only that they cannot explain.
On television, a woman shields her face to say
That child did nothing, nothing. Just sat in her car seat
As they drove slowly. We will gather
Next month when the peach trees blossom
To remember your mother, our rehearsed tributes
Pattering like rain upon that old-blood earth.

FENCES

Confirm the religion of property,
The doctrine of primogeniture.
This land is your land sing the penniless.

The herds of wildebeests
Cannot reach water. The great
Migrations are no more.

Ornamental wrought iron balconies
Contain the hooded women
Who donate their sons to history.

White pickets of cottages
Uphold hollyhocks and iris
In postcards of platitudes. Home

Is surrounded with great slabs
Of wooden privacy. Lie naked
In sunlight absorbing Vitamin D

And melanoma. This is the mansion
Of the inventor of barbwire
That tamed the west. In blizzards, cattle

Freeze on the hooks of prosperity.
Was Frost sarcastic or did he believe
Poems could enclose his intention

For posterity? Provide. Provide.
Good neighbors pound the posts
Slathered with creosote

To last for generations,
Securing the rails
That define boundaries.

GOOD NEWS

Cannot be trusted. The second day,
When the pathology arrives,
The doctor sheepish in a retraction.

The boys horsing around, celebrating
On a rooftop, six stories into the
Gape of pedestrians.

The winning filly that breaks down
A furlong past the wire.
When you tell me

I should be glad, I cross
Fingers and don the red dress of luck,
Though it is not becoming

With its hue of arterial blood.
While you think I should be dancing
With my hands full of money,

I foresee banks burning, a woman tripping
In the street, the road ragers
Shooting out the lights.

Swimmer

Australian crawl, side stroke, back stroke, breast stroke.
Plowing through the coastal currents or
Counting laps in the winter pool,
You think this is your medium.

Channel swimmer cloaked in grease or
Casual bather on a pebbled beach. Flutter
Kicking, body surfing where the great waves
Break on the reef.

In the amniotic ocean, you swam
And dove as the gill slits closed and you began
The slow ascent to breath.

Because you learned to breathe with every stroke,
Turning your head from the liquid kiss, you suppose
This element that you crave can love you back.

Flashing through depths, alert
For sharks or man o' war militias,
You think it simply takes determination
Like the woman who treads water for thirteen hours.

The riptide excites panic
As it carries you seaward with a rush.
Resisting, you forget
The parallel solution.

One inhalation
Can be the one that
Drowns you. Consider that
The first thing you learned was the
Dead man's float.

As a child, my family's menu consisted of two choices: take it or leave it.

—Buddy Hackett

Back Seat

The power poles race past,
Stabbing the wheat fields. Sometimes
She pretends she is on horseback
Jumping culverts and Burma Shave signs.

She can't read or the whirl
Will flatten her with sickness.
Smoke rings float toward
The windshield where her mother

Exhales incessantly. A busy factory
Crumpling packs of Camels. Her father sings
Off key, renditions of Stephen Foster—
"My Old Kentucky Home," "Jeanie With the Light Brown Hair."

Hers is reddish like machinery rusted
And discarded. An occasional stop
For a photo opportunity. The Rolleiflex suspends
From his neck like a dead animal.

Tripod set up in the overlook.
A waterfall in its constancy. He wants
Her in the foreground for perspective.
Look at the scenery, he commands

Once they attain the mountains.
A pine struggles with a cliff face.
Blanket of tiny flowers above the treeline.
She wants more than to oversee

What will be a slide in the projector.
The spark of her mother's lighter,
Then a staircase of smoke she might ascend
Into thunderheads that are moving in.

SITTING

With his pocket knife, he cut a plug
And stuck it in his jaw. The stream
Of tobacco juice brown as
Excrement shot into the brass spittoon
With such accuracy that I was both awed
And repelled.
Half blind from an explosion on the coal docks,
A scant pension let him sit
Through afternoons of the radio soaps
His woman loved. *Stella Dallas. How the World
Turns.* His favorite, *Just Plain Bill.*
He'd push the mower over sparse grass
In the backyard where a Tree of Heaven
Dropped its stinking pods. Pick up the
Pale turds that Laddie deposited.
That dog lived 15 years on bread crusts and
Rancid baloney. He wept digging
The grave in the vacant lot.
I sat on the porch steps observing
A city of red ants. I was the Lord Mayor.
Occasionally, I'd squash one to demonstrate
My powers. I admired how they hauled
A beetle like slaves who built the pyramids
In my book about the Pharaohs.
Sitting in the cellar by the boiler,
He told me about the mule teams
He drove in the copper mines in Butte.
How, at 12, he'd run away from beatings;
Later, how he'd ridden the rails
All over the western states. A stream
Of caramel juice hit the spittoon
With regularity. He wore suspenders
And a blue work shirt buttoned tight.
His shoes were heavy,
His black sweater on a hook by the back door.

Mostly he drank soup because part of his tongue
Had been sliced away—*Cancer,*
A fearful, whispered word. It didn't stop
The plug, the chaw, the spitting.
The pungent tobacco smell
That sat on Papa like his workman's cap
With a brim he tugged as he told me
The names of all his horses.

HANDS-ON TOOLS

A wooden box of his grandfather's hand tools,
Carefully kept. Hammers and saws,
Awl and auger. His dad's set of screwdrivers
And wrenches. Handed down.
He admired Norm's elaborate workshop
On *This Old House*, converted a corncrib
And granary in emulation: table saw,
Drill press, jigsaw, router, chain-
Saw, bandsaw, wood lathe, shaper, planer,
Sander. The shining display
Of workmanship he'd learned as a boy.
Small hands aligned with larger
Roughened hands. Thumbnails square
As the old-time nails that pegged
The floorboards. How the joists joined
In the balloon-framed house. The
Stair treads set, finials shellacked.
His dad and granddad,
Men who knew what
Making things meant.
His bandsaw sings the sawdust
Into a memory indispensable and true
As a spirit level. The old caution:
Measure twice,
Cut once.

LITTLE BIG HORN

I was his lieutenant in the war
Against my mother. On weekends, we went
To museums of armory, shields and
Battle-axes, or the historical society where Laocoön
And his children struggled
With a serpent. Where his photos of the
Vibrant city depicted busy
Wharves, the toxic river.
He gave me horses and poetry,
How to be observant and obstructive
With a grimly quiet resistance.
Their battles were silent—his strategy
A stalk-out to clubs where naked
Women posed or dunes where he could frame
The perfect tall grass captured
In its perfect sway.
Hers a crusade, novenas,
Litanies. A hierarchy of priests
Attended her parade
Of rosaries and missals.
Years later, when he'd surrendered
In a sick bed, wounded and confessing
The weapons of the weak would
Always conquer any man brought up
To honor a moral code. It seemed
A justification, how he'd sold out
For peace at last. I stood
Like Custer on the barren mound,
Ammunition gone, waving an
Empty pistol.
At the funeral home, she bargained
For a cheaper rate
Then laid his bones
In consecrated ground.

PODIATRY

The podiatrist operates on your big toe,
Removing the nail with what looks like
A pliers and then cauterizing the oozing bed
With caustic oil. He says in a week or so
You should be able to walk without
Agony. He tells you walking
Is essential to health. His parents were
Holocaust survivors. The day they walked
Out of the abandoned barracks,
Living skeletons, their feet
Wrapped in rags, what a day that was!
How they walked to the D.P. camps, walked
On ship decks, walked to the immense fortune
Of a son educated
To fix feet like yours. So walk!

Your toe, page of erasure,
A fat white grub. Underneath
It's all gore like the untold stories
Of the podiatrist's mother and father.
He has conjured from pictures what they suffered.
Suffering, he contends, must be endured
To heal. You can't bear
Weight on that foot yet. His eyeglasses
Glitter like frozen ponds
Over which the world must creep
Tentatively, step by cautious step.

Next week, you will walk
Into his surgery to expose
Tenderness, an unshelled
Toe. He's compelled to expunge
The carapaces his parents cowered under,
Tongues stuck to hard palates,
Roofs iced over,
Footprints bloodying the snow.

Science of the foot. Mechanics
Of walking. How a person is saved,
Escape accomplished.
A lowly procession of ingrown nails, bunions,
Plantar warts and fallen arches.
No foot, no horse, he says.

They walked from the boxcars
To be judged. The lame, the toddlers
Shunted to the ovens. His parents
Walked; they slaved in the quarries
Hauling baskets of stones. He's seen
The documentaries. His parents:
Their faces drawn and tight like
People whose feet hurt.

This good son soaks in remembrance,
Unbandaging your foot,
Which has improved. The profession he chose,
Foot doctor, seems vaguely comic.
Five little piggies crammed
In pointed spikes
The way they were jammed
In the ghettos or hiding
In an annex above the factory they owned
Before declared personas non grata,
People sewn with yellow stars.
He owns this history. Every patient
Whose foot he holds in accomplished hands
Will recollect it with
Every perfected stride.

GEOGRAPHY OF THE DREAM

We seek our houses, we swim, we fly, we lose
Our keys, misplace the car, find our beloved dead
Wearing fedoras and hats with veils.

We ride horses, we arrive in class
Unprepared, our notes missing.
We appear on the avenue of the naked.

We make excuses, solve delusions we are pursued
By spies. We climb scaffolds, panic in elevators.
We are not ourselves

Or we are young again and passionate.
The images dissolve in feelings so intense
We wake shuddering. We write down

What we can remember: The lover faceless and nameless.
The university of discovery.
The boiler room where bad things happen.

TRACED

In exchange for access, you agree to be
Followed. What you admire, briefly.
The dogs you like; the little stray
You stroked, then in dismay
Discovered an audience of fleas and ticks.
In the forest, you hoped to be
Hidden in the house of sweets
With a charged cell phone.
That's not how it works, said the witch
Lighting the oven. This is the risk
You take in obedience
To the principles of get and give.
An eye watches your house
From weather to weather. It zooms in
To a vertical view.
Anyone can find your address,
For a little money your life story.
Whatever you scatter can be traced.

MEASLES

A darkened room. Venetian blinds
Slatted like a stern mouth.
No reading. No coloring books
Or paper dolls. I shut my eyes
Reddened like the polka dots
Of my fevered body.
The doctor with his satchel
Of uselessness. Two weeks
Or longer. It's the hard
Measles.

Two infant boys born before my father
Died of it. They were both named
For their own father, an unlucky
Name as it turned out—he too would die
Young in a gunfight. They called my father
A different name. So names must
Matter. My own means Gift of God
According to my mother, who never wanted
Such a daughter, one spotted
With original sin who must be
Worried over, hot and sulky in the dark,
Demanding one more chapter.
My father's weary voice as Jim
Hides in the apple barrel
Listening for the thump of a peg leg.

Once a third of the tribes crawled
To the cooling waters where they expired.
I get better. A neighbor child
Loses smartness, burnt away in a conflagration
The way conifers on the mountain
Turned into ashy witches.

It was eradicated, almost, then someone got a notion
About vaccines and autism. A former Playmate proclaimed

And parents shrank from syringes. Spotted babies
Wail as the war between nonsense and evidence surges.

There's such a thing as herd
Immunity. The few protected
By the many. How penguins huddle
Against weather, changing places constantly
For the good of all.

Remember tetanus, smallpox, rabies,
Whooping cough, diphtheria,
Yellow fever, meningitis.
How graveyards held
Small headstones.

Age of enlightenment.
Lords of miracle: Lister, Pasteur,
Jenner, Finlay, Reed, Salk.

Yet in the forest where the children stray
The house of the witch still beckons.
People believe in angels, in green men from Mars,
That evolution is a lie, that the moon is a hologram,
That science is a devil's plot
Against the faith of conjecture.

LABOR DAY

At twelve, he drove a mule train
In Montana copper mines. He'd run off
From the Iowa farm where beatings were
The breakfast of an orphan. Men
Were hung for organizing. He was
A proud Union guy. Rode the rails
Till he and Henry landed
In the limestone quarries of Lemont
Where two Irish sisters took their eyes.

Seven kids, four lived. He labored
On the coal docks on Lake Calumet.
The mills blackened the sky
Over his clapboard house.
When his dog Laddie Buck died,
Tears crevassed his swarthy cheeks
As he dug the pit deep enough
For any sorrow.

Shovel: icon of labor.
In the snowstorm of '55
His heart burst as he hefted
That final sparkling load.

GLIMPSES

How a glimpse can be more circumspect
Than the long stare that dissembles
And reassembles, how shotgunned logic
Can miss less than a sharpshooter transfixed
On crosshairs.

How light and shadow glissaded
Under the pergola shawled with wisteria.
It was a moment—nothing was meant.
How a dragonfly hovered
Above the tide pool. You were a child then
Troubled with beauty and fright.

Look sideways to grasp the gist.
Close observation will put a spin
On everything when what you want
Is intimation. A whisper you can't
Quite make out but like the tone of.
The way a hand is raised in greeting
Or farewell.

THE NANAS

I printed the commanded letter
To the distant grandmother I'd met
Once when I was two and didn't
Remember, though I remember
Other things from that car trip. My father
Reading me *Little Black Sambo* or singing
"Dixie" and "Old Black Joe" as he headed back
South to his boyhood. My mother exhaling furiously,
Her cigarettes filling the Dodge with a miasma.
Later a cousin with blonde curls and a sand pail.
A lizard on a wall.

My mother referred to that grandmother
As Nana T. An imposter. My real Nana
Lived six blocks away in a house
Across from the slag pile.
She crocheted by the window and gave me
Peppermints. I liked to play
With her button jar and listen to her sing
"The Wearin' of the Green" and "Peg in a Low-backed Car."
My real Nana called me Joanie the way
People who liked me did.

That other grandmother, Nana T.,
Didn't like Catholics, my mother said.
I would be going to St. Felicitas though
My best friend Nancy would not.
Once on a Friday, I ate a baloney sandwich
At Nancy's house. The first meat
Of my revolution.

Nana T. never called me anything. She wrote
Letters to my father that began "Dear Son."
Her only surviving boy. Her five daughters
Each annoyed her in a separate fashion.
I learned that Nana T.'s husband

Was killed in a gunfight. How her own father
Rode with Morgan's Raiders, then roved the west
Trailing wives and children like chum
In dark waters. Nana T. shook off the Mormon
Suitors, then went back south
The way we did when I was little.
When my father was nine years old,
Nana T. gave him a gun. He shot a bird
And was sorry. She subscribed to New York
Papers, told him he'd be someone. Her family
Of generals and preachers,
Bible readers, whiskey drinkers, horse racing men.
She rode cow ponies when she was young in Texas.

Nana T. died never knowing
She was Nana T. In my letters I wrote
Grandmother. She wrote my father
That I seemed to be an intelligent girl.
The real Nana never made such judgments.
She loved me as she loved the white dog Laddie
Or all her lady friends or the Sacred Heart
Of Jesus or poor Stella Dallas on the radio.

Years later, sorting through the boxes
Of photographs, I pulled one out—
A woman on a porch looking serious.
It's you! My husband says, holding it up
Before me like a mirror. On the reverse, in pencil,
Margaret Wise Taylor. Nana T.
The Nana who never could forgive
My father for wedding that Yankee woman.
The Nana who never wrote back to me.

VALENTINE

The damselflies form a heart shape
In the wheel of their desire.

He clasps her thorax. She bends to
Admit him. The circuitry of their

Connection completed, they can hold
The pose for hours

Or, airborne, fly in tandem,
Their lacy wings a valentine.

We of heavy flesh and bone
Twine thick legs to hump and

Groan. Pant and grimace or dog-style
Deface lover from lover.

Earthbound, we will never hover,
Grounded in our meat.

BREAKING UP

That night in the car, having found her,
His voice shook with bad weather
Like the rain pouring over the windshield.

You could say she'd been abducted
Though she didn't think that.
She thought *How dare you.* When

He put the gun to her head,
It wasn't bravery when she said
Just stop. It was scorn;

It was the broken glass of their misadventure
Into his fantasy of possession,
Her fantasy of love. Neither authentic.

Seventeen and nineteen,
What could they possibly know?
They knew enough.

She had no use for drama, pushing away
The cold metal of his intention,
And he began to cry and she didn't care.

LIKE DREAMS

They disappear like dreams, these planes
That go off-course, undetectable, one moment
A speck on radar, then nothing,

Like waking and trying to remember
When all you have is pure emotion. Somewhere
In that ocean, uncharted, there might be

Wreckage. That's what happens
When love dissolves in flame, like plastic,
Leaving only the toxic odor.

Everyone is looking for evidence. Something
To surface, floating, or the ping of the black
Box. But it's all surrender. No one

Ever wants to hear your dream. The entire sea
Renounces the divisions imposed by chartmakers.
Bits and pieces of flotsam jog your memory.

It's another morning. You're up and at it.
The salt water calm and deep. Whatever went down
Or where, it doesn't matter.

MEMORIZING DARKNESS

They remembered how she lay all day
Facedown on the bed after the sheriff's knock
And then arose to reset the clock of her life.
Could she ever forget? Of course not.
Retold, the mind paints a scene
Even more vivid. How the cattle guard
Traps the wagon, the gunshots ringing.
And there he is running and firing,
His dark eyes wide as when they made love.

Memory: the stone door that locks on
An image forever, a bloodstain that can't
Be scrubbed. The lies we're told: how home is where,
When you go there, they have to take you in.
Or that you can't go home. As if anything
Will ever be the same. As if a stall means safety.
Ghost horses screaming in the flames.

THE KEY FOR THE LOST

Small, silver as a minnow, so insignificant
I can't believe how you hold it up
Like a trophy, like the key to a 400-million-dollar
Lottery. You're outside looking in.
Everyone is still alive.
I remember Dad putting on his rainbow boots
And leaving. That must have been in 1983.
He hasn't been back, but surely he might be.
That's what the key is for, I say,
Holding out my hand. So when they return,
All those who are missing,
I can let them in.

Now It's Time

We pour into the sleeping world
Like people boarding a train.
The station dark with hurry.
Suitcases on wheels like companion animals.
The roar of the resting engines as they gather
Intent. We find our tight compartment, slide
Onto the facing benches. It is God's voice
At the door of dream. We cross the trestle to enter
An avalanche shed. The elevation is eleven thousand
Feet. *Breathe, breathe,* I tell you. Even in the dream,
I know I'm dreaming. A house I've lived in for years
In this alternate existence is familiar as the beautiful
World of awakening, a world that quakes with relief
As pursuers vanish behind the pillars of Morphia.
I am overwhelmed with grief, a blizzard of excuses,
How we rolled along the river where salmon leaped
In the dance of life and death. I don't want to leave
This earth. Exhausted with the burdens of love and need,
I could lie here half-dreaming while the clocks
Cry out like roosters, red priests of sunrise.
I am planted like a garden, every seed another lie
That has made life bearable. The brakes shriek, gears
Grab steel. I forgive all my failings and yours.

EVERYTHING HAS TO COME TO AN END SOMETIME.

—L. FRANK BAUM
(*THE MARVELOUS LAND OF OZ*)

SITTING UNDER A POPLAR AT PLEASANT HILL, SHAKER VILLAGE

That they adored frenzy seems odd
This hot July afternoon with intermittent
Breeze stirring phlox and wild
Mustard. Whitewashed bricks hide
Cool, dark interiors. Flagstone paths
And picket fences, cliché of
Ordinary bliss not crazed
Dancing the rivulets of nerve to
Celestial sensation.

       The rest was pure
Domestic labor: spinning wool,
Tanning leather, baking loaves,
Preserving, coopering, sacking paper packets
With seeds of their good faith.
Men and women climbing separate staircases
To the ecstatic dual face of God, never halting
To yearn or touch.

       The rescued orphans bide their time
Dreaming of cities, whiskey, laughter. Most
Have left; the gaudy world inched closer
Waving flags and pistols, loaded dice
And gypsy skirts.

This simple life is best
Glossolalia, shaking with
The spirit of the two-sexed god. Each woman clasps
The man within herself. That man
Who, like a ghost, nods
Across the pasture, reins around his neck,
Eyes unbridled. Her skirts dip and rise
In quiet dancing steps.

       On her hip, a staved basket
Of apples he had picked. Sleeving sweat from his brow,
His shirt woven by her. And never

A word passes
Except in glorifying prayer.
At last, the final twelve
Apostles of vanished order trade heritage
For lifelong care. Each twirling, virginal, to that
Spare grave.

The easy wind dandles my hair. In the meadow, a cow bellows,
Birds jabber past, the garden hums with insects and shaking petals.
Overhead, the sun sets its bright stain against a clarity of blue,
Horizon-wide, blotting a chaos of countless stars.

Here's what they knew; here's what they denied:
There is nothing celibate in this luxurious air.

The Heart of the Woodlot

In the thick of the woodlot,
Ancient corn pickers rust
Into oblivion, wooden parts
Rotting, becoming one with
Blowdown and scrub,
Attended by oak and hickory,
A bastion of ash, mulberry, wild
Cherry, prolapse of branch and leaf
Secluding the discards. Manure spreaders
Shredding slats, wheels
Occluded with raspberry canes.
Bits and pieces, the gravestone of a
Dog whose etched name blurs. A hidden
History of the useless and broken
Hauled to rest unseen, unspoken, claimed
By grapevine and bittersweet.
Simulacrum of a simple farmer's
Angkor Wat. Artifacts of age and
Industry. Grungy leather horse collars,
The harrow's teeth set into earth
In a grinning rictus, a metal seat
From a tractor pierced into the
Trunk of a box elder.
All that was unfit
For the annual burn pile mustered
Like old soldiers bivouacked in greenery.

When the Birds Vanished

They were gone suddenly.
A silence in the oaks.
A stillness haunting the air
As if a breath could not be taken.
They didn't wait around
Hoping for the visa,
Not believing such things
Could happen. When they set off
It was night. They took the baggage
They could carry, tramped through fields
Until they reached the mountains
Where the guide held out his hand
For money. High overhead in dawnlight,
The shadow of a cross
Threatened their passage.
They had to set down what had
Grown too heavy. Even then
They imagined returning: the silver and lace
Of the apartment on the boulevard
Where their children played while the elders
Decided. The hawks filled the sky,
Soaring the thermals. When their ship was
Refused in port after port, they continued to hope
Past reason. Hadn't they flown
When the branches filled with
The hunched shoulders of idols,
The songless ones, sharp-eyed
As snipers? O, they left all right.
The bread unsliced on the table
And the silence, the silence.

THE DARKER ANGELS OF THE IMAGINATION

Angels fall from ambition like politicians.
They conceal the dark secrets of their stony
Hearts. Pay off the mercenaries, pay tribute
To the noble lord of destiny, the thunder
Wielder, auspicious ghost, the sperm
That salts the seas to exalt beauty.
The crucified or the transposed.
Lord Krishna in his bee form,
Christ among the lepers.
Someone always hopes to supplant
The overseers. Once slaves can read
They write the bible of justice, not mercy.
Devils are troubled. Like abused children
Who intend to get even, they fork souls
Into the hell of self-consciousness. A father
Beats his son into a bishop. So love
Is intermediate, a planetary equivalent.
When dragons fell into songbirds' nests
To hatch a feathered dynasty, belief
Obtained authority. The devil is interested
In the pure-in-heart. An innocence
That can be tempted.

NO TROPHIES OF THE SUN

After Hart Crane

Splashes of light beneath the trees
Migrate like birds in a forecast
Of instinct and pressing time

That repeats itself like words
Misunderstood in the common tongue
Of dailyness. What we expect

Is what we think we earn,
So no surprise that flowers overnight
Will take us in white arms

As if engaged with lilies.
The coffin-haunted blooms
Engulf the rooms of people

Who dust the shelves and pour
Coffee into morning mugs, who wait
For each day to imitate the other.

JOYRIDING TO NIGHTFALL

A house on a hill awaits the faithful—
That's us, redhanded and sorrowful,
Our knives, our handkerchiefs. Bless
The storm skirting the horizon to sweep
The harvest into baskets of wind.
Here we are joyriding in stolen
Dune buggies or jeeps, laughing
At the invisible charts of history,
Stories abolished in the bibles
Of desire: Mythmaking lions
Prowling the desert, wizards with silver turbans
Sitting in shopping malls, all the wrinkled women
Washing clothes in the foul rivers; the onion-topped
Churches, pagodas of the magnificent,
Caramel arroyos or the catacombs
Where skulls of monks shine
In a darkness that will summer in our bones.

ZIKA

The skull enlarges to furnish the dream house
Where the spirit resides,
Unlike the belly that simply hungers
Or the mouth where words propagate
In a calendar of saints.

The passage to life must involve
Agony. The infant head crowning
Like a juggernaut rolling through the narrow alley
While the acolytes scream and sacrifice themselves.

Support the head, the mother is told.
This is how to hold the beloved:
Gently, firmly, with purpose.
Carry it like a basket of lilies.
See how the eyes meet yours.
You will never escape this moment.

A blueprint in the shape of a tear.
The way a wildfire
Could ignite from one sky-borne stroke
Of a passing thunderhead.
Our place on the spectrum
Of mercy or destruction. A room
Decorated in bravura taste, papered with the
Beautiful question of existence, the plentiful doors
Opening as if, beyond the stars,
There might be more than darkness.

TIME

The time it takes to savor
A small bowl of grapes
Or even less to boil the water
For tea; enough time to starve
The brain of oxygen, those few
Minutes of blessing denied. Father,
One eye open, one eye shut.
The respirator breathing like an
Extinct animal with useless enormous
Fangs. It carries the weight
Of my father's destiny, which has already
Been decided. In that short time
Before the paddles were applied,
He hung in space like a planet,
Already, the neurons frozen, the memories
Erased from the book of his existence.
Consider the moment the girl,
Intent on a selfie, stepped back
For a more perfect angle and fell
A thousand feet into the canyon.
The moment between singing
And the explosion, the café reduced
To ash. The trigger and the trajectory,
The red circle on the child's forehead.

GRACE READING AT HOWTH BAY

—Sir William Orpen (1878-1931)

The sea is grey like the scudding clouds and the pebbled shale.
Her dress is grey with shadows. Her hat is black.
You can tell how the wind is blowing the way her skirt
Flings itself toward the rock-studded waters.
The painter has provided a book.
We might assume from its lack of heft that it's a thin
Volume of poetry: Keats or Rossetti. Her golden hair
Is caught in a net or a snood. She steadies her hat
That the breeze threatens, her eyes cast down,
Appropriate to a sonnet or possibly
An elegy. The implausible scene: a beach wind-riven
And stony. Offshore rain is moving in. She isn't dressed
For weather. The Great War has not yet come
Like a gale off the Irish Sea. The artist will be known
For paintings of dead soldiers, generals, battlefields,
Prisoners of war, the open grave of the Somme, a coffin
Covered with the Union Jack.
But none of this has happened. Foreshadowed
By small bayonets of whitecaps, she stands
Windswept by the pewter bay,
Peering at the pages she may find
Tiresome or endearing.

Cast

The colt can't get his legs under him,
Jammed tight against the planks
Of the stall. Cast,
Eyes rolling, nostrils bloodied where he's
Scraped himself thrusting to revolve
A solid girth. Shoes flashing a bright
Iron, breath in heaves, sawdust
Caking each gasp. We strive
To get a rope on cannon bones and haul
Him free of constriction, kicking
Like a mad king at the ungiving wall,
Till finally he's up, shuddering, wet as if a
Rainstorm had pinned him.

Once I saw a horse die like that.
I was ten. Two men wrestled the boards
To give him room. The horse struggled,
Then nothing. His big heart broke.
In the shine of his still glistening eye,
I could see my own reflection.
He was a pretty chestnut with a star.
His name was Arrow. I didn't cry.
I just stood, waiting.
It seemed like something
Should happen, something I didn't
Know about yet. *Kid*, one man said,
These thoroughbreds are born
Committing suicide.
An old cliché, but I didn't know that yet either.
I thought there must be more to it.

DEPORTATIONS

Saturday mornings, I wake
To the growl of the mower going past
Our bedroom windows: a man hunched
In a hoodie over the controls swerving
Around the evergreen and lilac bushes.

Two years ago, I looked hard and said,
Inquiringly, *You're not Isidro*. He
Laughed. *Isidro went back to Mexico.*
I'm José. I felt like an actor
In a bad cliché.

The year of drought. The grass turned brown
As grocery bags. My neighbor said
José is cleaning stalls over on Bahr Road
A boarding stable where girls in hard hats
And shining boots jump horses over hurdles.
José forks manure, spreads straw,
Breaks hay bales into flakes.

The rains return. José
Has a new truck, two mowers, two helpers,
Jorge and Hector. One smiles, the other stern,
Intent upon the task as he mows down
Our daylilies. José presents his bill.
The price has risen. *You should*
Warn us. He grins: a capitalist,
Entrepreneur. His new business card.

Two months now. He never mulched
The leaves, never took the leftover shingles
We said he could have. His phone
Rings and rings. We still owe him
For October.

At the Window (1881)

—Hans Olaf Heyerdahl

If a woman is to pose
On a balcony overlooking
A city of roofs,
She needs a book
That will lie open in her lap,
The unread words configuring
Grief or remorse.

She looks away
As the painter hollows
Her cheekbones, leans her elbow
On the wrought-iron railing
To prophesy sorrow,
Casts her gaze down, ignoring
The frayed pages
With their sonnets or love stories.

A book accessorizes
The forlorn or insoluble,
How the woman is made to look away
From directives as the brush
Dresses her in blue silk,
Knots a ribbon in her hair.

THE BEAT

The world's in motion. That's the elegance
Of a girl's blonde ponytail posting
Upon the palomino whose pale
Plume keeps the cadence of the pace.
Shadowed down the bridal path,
Beneath the overarching elms,
That's the vast tick-tock
Of a city's clock. Presence of
Pedestrians with their swinging purses
Or backpacks who know the meter
Of the vanished stars that set their hearts
Upon the scale where grace notes glissade
Into the big, imponderable chords.
Heel and toe. The step dance
Batters the wooden stage
And a dog's tail wags furiously
In acclamation of a visitor.
What you might think is senescence
Is simply the pause between the beats
That commands attention as you await
The other legendary shoe,
Then the bed creaking to the bodies'
Midnight rhythm in the rain or the squeaking
Mouse within the wall that wakes you
To your own heart pounding
In your ear, a tympanum. It's true
The body keeps on going after dying,
Bones rattling with each shift of clay.
There must be bells ringing in the chamber
Of the prime minister as he composes
The epitaph of his final office.

Before Surgery

Saddle the horse of morning.
The day of the dead approaches.
Sugar skulls grin from the shelves.
In the blind canyon, shadow
Congeals where the trapped boy
Cut off his arm with a penknife.
The horse whinnies and rears.
The old coin of the sun is rubbed
To a blur, the clouds herded
Like distracted cattle. In the valley
Knives await like Indians atop the rimrocks.
Smoke signals spell the name
On the waiver that permits
Slow fires, skinning knives,
The ghost dance.

THE WAVE

The wave that drowns the Afghan boy
Escaping to a new life is the wave
That lifts the barge with its cargo of flowers
From the casket of a reef
And is the wave in the hair of the girl
Who dances in a rave in a slum in Edinburgh
Or the wave for which a boy with a surfboard lurks
And the wave that crashes on a beach
In an old movie to signify
Censored passion. The wave
Of starlings in their murmuration
Erases the horizon. That's the wave
That takes a village out to sea.

He Plans His Funeral

There are children of thirteen planning their funerals.
The gang slogans that will be inscribed
And shouted at the wake, the hand signals displayed
With vigor and an emotion that is partly
Theatrical and partly realized
As the procession of mourners
Wearing T-shirts printed with his face bends
To inspect his closed eyes, his fingers folded
Over folded bills. Someone tucks a toy gun
Next to the silken pillow where a teddy bear
Has been snugged by his mother
Who is stone-faced remembering his instruction
Not to cry. He is so young.
At the site where he fell bleeding
There's a pyramid of stuffed toys,
Pastel as angels, and signs with RIP
In elaborate capitals designed by boys
Who don't know the Latin.
He has it all laid out
For the undertaker of his final wishes:
How he will lie in state in the storefront chapel
On a street as grim and angry
And excitable as he was
Carrying the small flag of revenge
For the only nation he belonged to.
See him now as he wanted to be seen
In the white wedding suit he never got to wear
For the girl he never got to touch.

BEQUEST

Sweetheart. Love song. Model of inefficiency
Like the nuthatch who grabs one seed
And caches it in the oak. In the event I'm gone,
I leave you this reminder. I have always dreaded
Disfigurement—the man without a nose,
His sinuses clogged with cancer, like the man
Without a country at sea with no friends.
These are metaphors for what's coming
Over the pass, then the switchbacks
Gearing down and the brakes squawking
Like jays, birds of plunder. Icarus wanted
What has come so easily to us. Take off your shoes.
Be scanned like the man who can't stop coughing
In the theater of consequences. Hold out your hands;
Someone will give you alms if you happen to be
In the proper country, one where charity is legislated.
Not here. Not here where finders are keepers,
Where the zoo of unfortunates attracts the strollers
Who point and jeer. The child in the arms of the
Gorilla. King Kong on the pinnacle of what was
The highest building. The empire of grandiosity.
See how I veer into philosophy when all I meant
Was to leave you some token, some clue
For the scavenger hunt—what you must bring back,
What you must prove. Oh, listen,
You don't need to prove anything. Forgive me.
The rain keeps falling; it affects my mood.
This testament I want to leave you
As if I had any wisdom, as if what anyone says
Could avert the finality. I wanted to tell you something
Hopeful, not how scar tissue cannot be anesthetized,
Not that everyone must suffer the worst fear—
Rats in the mask and all that. This was intended
To console you. I wanted to write a song
Like a country road with a cabin and smoke
Rising from a chimney. I wanted to tell you

No one is cruel on purpose,
But that's a lie. It's always purpose
That drives the truck backfiring
And gearing up for something:
That cliff. That pedestrian.
History's a blink. You occupy
Only one space surrounded by your shadow
And then, without light, you are nowhere.
But what I really meant was that feeling exists:
Why would anyone live otherwise,
Or wish you well, all of you
Now and to come. Especially you,
Sweetheart. Love song. I can't seem to stop this
Agony. When did I become preoccupied
With goodness, that outlaw spirit
To which I brought tribute? Heads. Hearts.
Bags of the stolen. You ought to laugh,
But who laughs as the hood is fastened,
The noose tightened? Once we believed
Artifice trumps reality. We believed
A lot of things before breakfast
Like the White Queen in the woodcut.
Prisoners of jabberwocky and the Dickensian
Mills, listen: we are orphans.
Our beloved ones are ghosts now.
In the book of maybes, there's an asterisk
For the footnote that was our lives.

A Canticle for the Bereaved

Like casseroles or potted plants,
Poems to ease grief,
Booklets of psalms and lilies
Or a rainbow road where dogs and cats
Await those who have passed
From master to ghost.

Like crossing fingers to avert the evil eye
Or telling hangman jokes,
The bereaved held at arms length
In the hug of schadenfreude.

Not knowing what to say, friends tell
Their own grim stories. An Irish wake
With its complements of Guinness
And Bushmills to insulate
The living from the dead.

THE BIBLE OF A DOG

Staring at my chicken sandwich,
She suddenly shows her wolf face,
Eyes fierce with desire. Pushes in too close.
I say *Enough of that!* She regains the composure
Of her training. How repetition processed
In the circuits of the brain
Rewires ambition to seize and swallow.
She offers her paw for nail-trimming,
The once-refused manicure accepted
By dint of over-and-over, the conditioning
We believe we are immune to. Free
Will and intellect. The bible of a dog
Is *sit* and *stay* and *fetch*. Surely, God
Asks no more of us than that.

ACKNOWLEDGMENTS

Abbey: "Diner"
The Alembic: "Arson"
Black Fox Literary Magazine: "Like Dreams"
Broadkill Review: "The Darker Angels of Imagination"
Boxcar Poetry Review: "Bequest"
The Cape Rock: "He Plans His Funeral"
Carnival: "Oblique," "When the Saints Go Marching"
Caveat Lector: "Opossum"
Comstock Review: "Migraine," "Voyageur"
Cypersoleil: "Glimpses"
First Literary Review—East: "February Thaw"
Four Chambers: "Before the Weather Moves Upon Us"
F(r)iction: "Eve of the Day"
Full of Crow: "Leap"
Furious Gazelle: "Podiatry"
Gargoyle: "Floating"
Glint: "A World of Sadness"
Gnarled Oak: "Geography of the Dream"
Homestead Review: "Composing the Essay," "Little Big Horn,"
    "Power," "Signature Rerum"
Iodine Poetry Journal: "The Heart of the Woodlot"
Kudzu: "The Old Feral Cat"
Little Patuxent Review: "Kneecapped"
Loch Raven Review: "Messages from the Latitude of Illness,"
    "The Wave"
Lost Coast: "Labor Day"
Manhattanville Review: "Swimmer," "No Trophies of the Sun"
Midnight Lane Boutique: "The Beat"
Midwestern Gothic: "Ice Storm in December"
Misfitmagazine: "Cast," "Gator," "Padraig," "The Nanas,"
    "The Squirrel," "Tulips"
Muddy River Review: "Good News," "Presence"
The new renaissance: "Sitting Under a Poplar at Pleasant Hill,
    Shaker Village"
New Verse News: "Measles"
One: "Now It's Time"
Plainsongs: "Joyriding to Nightfall"

Poppy Road: "Before Surgery," "Overdrive"

Prick of the Spindle: "The Wolves Need You"

Pyrokinetics: "Breaking Up," "Nashville"

Red Earth: "Lamb"

Red River Review: "Deportations"

Schuylkill Valley Journal: "Blackflies," "Speaking to Bees,"
    "Valentine"

Shark Reef: "Mites"

Sow's Ear: "Back Seat"

Stray Branch: "Once," "Rime"

Tar River Review: "Stand Up for the Stupid and Crazy"

THAT Literary Review: "Memorizing Darkness"

Third Wednesday: "Grace Reading at Howth Bay," "When the Birds
    Vanished"

Tipton Poetry Journal: "The Bible of a Dog"

Turtle Island Review: "So It Goes"

Vayavya: "Wasp"

Verse-Virtual: "Hands-On Tools," "The Key for the Lost," "Reflections
    After Midnight," "At the Window," "Photos Found in Camera,"
    "Traced"

Whale Road: "January Fog"

Wilderness House: "Laniakea—Immeasurable Heavens," "Sitting,"
    "A Canticle for the Bereaved"

ABOUT FUTURECYCLE PRESS

FutureCycle Press is dedicated to publishing lasting English-language poetry books, chapbooks, and anthologies in both print-on-demand and Kindle ebook formats. Founded in 2007 by long-time independent editor/publishers and partners Diane Kistner and Robert S. King, the press incorporated as a nonprofit in 2012. A number of our editors are distinguished poets and writers in their own right, and we have been actively involved in the small press movement going back to the early seventies.

The FutureCycle Poetry Book Prize and honorarium is awarded annually for the best full-length volume of poetry we publish in a calendar year. Introduced in 2013, our Good Works projects are anthologies devoted to issues of universal significance, with all proceeds donated to a related worthy cause. Our Selected Poems series highlights contemporary poets with a substantial body of work to their credit; with this series we strive to resurrect work that has had limited distribution and is now out of print.

We are dedicated to giving all of the authors we publish the care their work deserves, making our catalog of titles the most diverse and distinguished it can be, and paying forward any earnings to fund more great books.

We've learned a few things about independent publishing over the years. We've also evolved a unique, resilient publishing model that allows us to focus mainly on vetting and preserving for posterity poetry collections of exceptional quality without becoming overwhelmed with bookkeeping and mailing, fundraising activities, or taxing editorial and production "bubbles." To find out more about what we are doing, come see us at www.futurecycle.org.

THE FUTURECYCLE POETRY BOOK PRIZE

All full-length volumes of poetry published by FutureCycle Press in a given calendar year are considered for the annual FutureCycle Poetry Book Prize. This allows us to consider each submission on its own merits, outside of the context of a contest. Too, the judges see the finished book, which will have benefitted from the beautiful book design and strong editorial gloss we are famous for.

The book ranked the best in judging is announced as the prize-winner in the subsequent year. There is no fixed monetary award; instead, the winning poet receives an honorarium of 20% of the total net royalties from all poetry books and chapbooks the press sold online in the year the winning book was published. The winner is also accorded the honor of being on the panel of judges for the next year's competition; all judges receive copies of all contending books to keep for their personal library.

www.ingramcontent.com/pod-product-compliance
Lightning Source LLC
Chambersburg PA
CBHW072359090426
42741CB00012B/3087